FOOD & FEASTS

with the

Vikings

Hazel Mary Martell

Wayland

FOOD & FEASTS

Titles in the series

A ZOË BOOK

© 1995 Zoë Books Limited

Devised and produced by
Zoë Books Limited
15 Worthy Lane
Winchester
Hampshire SO23 7AB
England

First published in Great Britain in 1995 by
Wayland (Publishers) Ltd
61 Western Road, Hove
East Sussex BN3 1JD

British Library Cataloguing in Publication Data

Martell, Hazel Mary
 Food and Feasts with the Vikings
 I. Title
 394. 12094809021

ISBN 0-7502-1133-4

Printed in Italy by Grafedit SpA.
Design: Jan Sterling, Sterling Associates
Picture Research: Victoria Sturgess
Maps: Gecko Limited
Production: Grahame Griffiths

Photographic acknowledgments

The publishers wish to acknowledge, with thanks, the following photographic sources:

Antikvarisk - topografiska arkivet, Stockholm 3, 4, 13t, 14t&b, 17br, 23tl, 24l; Archäologisches Landesmuseum, Schloss Gottorf 13br; Arnamagnaean Institute, Reykjavik 10b; British Library, London 10t, 19b; C.M.Dixon 5t, 9t&b, 11t, 12b, 13bl, 15t, 20t&b, 21b; Robert Harding Picture Library / Matyn Chillmaid 6t, / Richard Elliott 7t; Michael Holford 8t, 21t, 24r; Kulturen, Lund 6b, 18b; Nationalmuseet, Copenhagen 12t, 25b; Trondheim University 11b; University of Oslo 7b, 17t, 23tr&b, 25t; University Library, Utrecht 5b; York Archaeological Trust Picture Library title page, 8b, 15b, 16t&b, 17bl, 18t, 19t.

Cover: C.M.Dixon top right; Michael Holford top left; Nationalmuseet, Copenhagen bottom left; University of Oslo bottom right; York Archaeological Trust Picture Library centre.

The publishers have made every effort to trace the copyright holders, but if they have inadvertently overlooked any, they will be pleased to make the necessary arrangement at the first opportunity.

Contents

Introduction

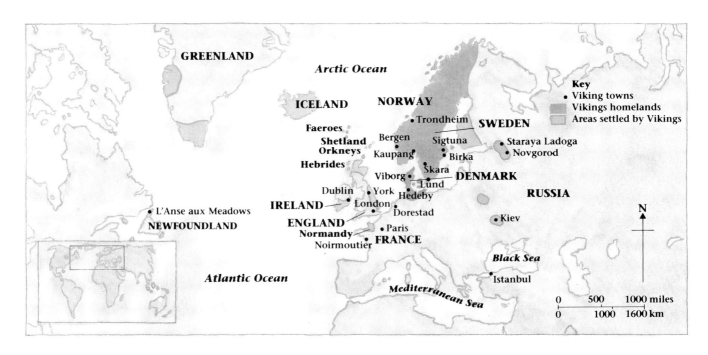

GREENLAND
Arctic Ocean
ICELAND   NORWAY
Faeroes
Shetland   Bergen   Sigtuna   SWEDEN
Orkneys   Kaupang   • Birka   • Staraya Ladoga
Hebrides   • Novgorod
           Viborg • Skara DENMARK
Dublin • York Lund
IRELAND London Hedeby   RUSSIA
ENGLAND   • Dorestad
• L'Anse aux Meadows Normandy • Kiev
NEWFOUNDLAND   Noirmoutier • Paris FRANCE
                                     N
Atlantic Ocean   Black Sea
              Mediterranean Sea • Istanbul
           0   500   1000 miles
           0   1000 1600 km

Key
• Viking towns
Vikings homelands
Areas settled by Vikings

△ The Viking Age lasted about 300 years. This map shows the Vikings' homelands and the places where they settled during that time.

▽ Wood carvings give us a good idea of what the Vikings looked like. This head of a Viking warrior comes from Sigtuna in Sweden.

The Vikings came from the lands we call Denmark, Norway and Sweden. Their **ancestors** lived by farming. About 1200 years ago, however, the population began to increase and by the 790s there was not enough good farmland to grow food for everybody.

Some Vikings then looked for new ways to make a living. They were adventurous by nature and, as most of them lived by the sea, they were also excellent shipbuilders. Their **longships** could be sailed or rowed in shallow water as well as on the open sea. Many Vikings set out to find new lands overseas.

The earliest Viking adventurers were robbers, or raiders, who attacked **monasteries** on the coast of England. Their first recorded raid was on the monastery at Lindisfarne in 793. Many more raids followed, not only in England but also in Ireland, Scotland, Wales, the Netherlands, France, Germany, Spain and Italy. At that time, very few people except **monks** could read or write. Naturally, the

The Viking alphabet was called the *Futhark* after the first six letters in it (*th* counted as one letter). There were only 16 letters altogether. The language was difficult to read as well as to write, because there was not a letter for every sound in the language.

△ The Viking runes on this stone say 'Estrid had this stone erected in memory of Osten, her husband, who went to Jerusalem and died in Greece'.

monks did not have anything good to say about the Vikings.

Now, however, **archaeologists** have found evidence to show that the Vikings were not just violent raiders. Many Vikings travelled long distances, buying and selling goods such as silk and jewellery. They were traders. Others settled as farmers in places where they had earlier raided or traded. Some Vikings sailed to Iceland and Greenland. Others visited North America, but their attempts to settle there failed.

Reading and writing was difficult for the Vikings. Their alphabet was made up of stick-like letters, called **runes**, which could be carved on to stone, metal or wood. This took a long time and written information was not easy to carry around. Most information was passed on by word of mouth. The Viking adventure stories, or **sagas**, which were written down in the 13th century, tell us about Viking feasts. However, no Viking recipes have survived. Almost everything we know about Viking food comes from archaeological evidence.

'. . .The Vikings laid everything to waste. They trampled the holy places with dirty feet, dug up the altars and seized all the treasures of the holy church. They killed some of the brothers. Some they took away with them in chains. Many they drove out, naked and loaded with insults, and some they drowned in the sea. . .'

Simeon of Durham's description of the Viking raid on Lindisfarne in AD 793.

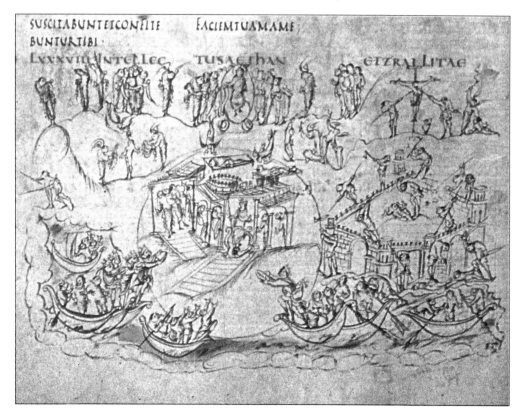

◁ This picture was drawn by a monk in a book called the *Utrecht Psalter*. It shows his idea of a Viking attack on a city in Europe.

Farming and food in the countryside

▷ In Norway, Denmark and Sweden, most Viking farms were on land which is still used for farming. In Iceland, however, some farms were abandoned in Viking times and never lived in again.

Archaeologists have dug out, or **excavated**, the site of one farm at Stong. The longhouse has been reconstructed from the evidence they found there. Wood was scarce in Iceland, so the house was built from blocks of grass and earth, known as turf.

A Viking farm

Most Vikings lived on farms in the countryside. They had to grow or make everything they needed, including food for their animals, so they spent a lot of time working on their land.

Cheese, milk and other **dairy produce** played a large part in the Vikings' diet. All farmers kept cattle, and most of them also kept pigs, sheep, goats, hens and geese for food. When the animals had been killed for their meat, their skins were treated, or tanned, into leather for clothes and household goods. Sheep's wool was spun and woven into cloth, while the feathers from the geese and hens were used to stuff pillows and mattresses.

▽ Most of the equipment used in Viking dairies was made from wood, like this cheese-drainer.

The main building on the farm was the **longhouse**, where the family lived. It was usually built of wood and had a roof which was **thatched** with straw or reeds. There was a barn, or byre, to shelter the animals in the hard winters. Iron tools

▷ As in Viking times, Norwegians today farm along the shores of the inlets, or *fjords*.

Viking society was divided into three groups – *jarls*, *karls* and *thralls*. *Jarls* were wealthy landowners and usually had a lot of power. *Karls* were also quite wealthy and often owned their own farms. If they had no land, they could work for a friend or relation and still be a free man. *Thralls* were slaves who had no rights, but they could earn their freedom if they worked hard. If a *karl* became very poor, he could become a *thrall* to make sure he had at least food and shelter, until the time when he could buy back his freedom.

were made or mended in the **smithy**. If the farmer owned a longship or other boat, there might be a boat-shed to keep it in.

Around the longhouse was a garden where the Vikings grew vegetables such as cabbages, leeks, carrots, peas and beans. They often grew herbs such as mustard, horseradish and mint to add flavour to their food. There was probably a small orchard with apple trees and plum trees. Beyond the garden were the fields in which barley, oats, wheat or rye – the **cereal crops** – were grown. These fields were sometimes surrounded by stone walls to stop the animals from trampling the crops. There were also meadows in which grass was grown. It was cut and dried for hay to feed the animals in winter. The work on the farm was usually done by the family, but on the larger farms there were probably also slaves, known as *thralls*. They helped with the heavy and unpleasant jobs, such as spreading **manure** on the fields in the early spring.

◁ Many Viking farmers made their own tools from iron and wood. They cut the grain crops with **sickles**. The grass for hay was cut with a **scythe**. Tools like these were still being used on farms at the beginning of the 20th century.

The farming year

△ This ploughing scene is from the *Bayeux Tapestry*. It was made more than 900 years ago, to tell the story of the Norman Conquest of England in 1066. The Normans (or 'Northmen') were descended from a group of Vikings who had helped the king of France to defend his country from other Vikings. These Vikings were given land in France in 911. The Normans who invaded England were very different from their Viking ancestors, but their farming methods were very similar.

Spring was a busy time for everybody on a Viking farm if they were to have enough to eat for the following year. Before any crops could be planted, the fields had to be ploughed. The children then removed any stones which the plough had brought to the surface. After this, the farmer sowed the seeds of barley, wheat, rye or oats which had been saved from the previous harvest. Once the seeds started to grow, the children were kept busy again. They

◁ Viking women spent a long time each day grinding grain on round stones called *querns*. They poured the grain through a hole in the top, then turned the top stone round and round with the handle. This squashed the grain between the two stones and eventually turned it into flour. Sometimes bits of the stone were ground in, too, and these wore down the Vikings' teeth when they were eating bread!

△ As well as mending their boats in winter, the Vikings used tools like these to make carts and sledges for moving things around on their farms. They made barrels, buckets and other containers out of wood, for storing food and drink. They probably also made furniture for their houses, but very little of it has survived.

pulled out the weeds and chased the birds away. At the same time, the vegetables were planted in the gardens and manure was spread on the hayfields to help the grass to grow.

As the weather became warmer, the sheep and cattle were taken away from the farm to summer pastures, or *shielings*. This meant that all the grass in the fields around the farm could be cut for hay in the early summer. After haymaking, there was a quiet time before the crops were ripe enough to harvest. This was when many of the men set out on raiding or trading adventures. The women ran the farms during this time.

The grain harvest in early autumn was a very busy time, and all the men tried to be back by then. Everyone helped to cut and harvest the crops and to take the grain back to the farmyard. Some of the grain was set aside, to plant for the next year's crop. The rest was **threshed** to separate the hard seed cases, or **chaff**, from the grain. The grain was then stored until it was needed. It might be ground into flour or used for making beer.

As the weather turned cold again, the farmers had to decide how many animals they could feed over the winter. There was not enough hay to feed them all, so the weakest ones were killed to provide meat for the family.

Winters were long, dark and cold in the Viking homelands. It was impossible to work out of doors. Winter was not an idle time, however. The men made and mended tools and kept the boats in good repair, while the women were kept busy spinning and weaving cloth, making clothes and feeding their families.

▽ This wooden food container was found at a Viking farmhouse in Iceland. The owner carved a design on the lid.

▽ When archaeologists excavate a site, they take samples of the soil back to their laboratories. There they try to find out more about the site in the past.

This soil is passed through sieves to separate out all the fragments of bones, shells and seeds. These are then examined and identified, with the help of a powerful microscope.

These remains give us clues about what people ate in the past. They also tell us something about the plants and animals that lived on a particular site.

△ A reconstruction of a town house at *Jorvik* which shows the kinds of food the Vikings ate and stored.

Obtaining food

Most houses in Viking towns were long and narrow. The narrow end of the house faced on to the street. Behind the house there was usually a workshop and a store-room and, behind this, there was a small yard or garden. Many people kept a pig or two, for meat. Others kept a goat, which would provide them with milk to drink or to make into cheese or butter. The yard could also be used for growing vegetables such as carrots, parsnips, celery, peas and beans. Herbs might also be grown there, and perhaps an apple tree. Many people also kept hens and geese, but these were allowed to wander in the streets. They fed on the piles of rubbish and on the many weeds that grew there.

The grain crops were grown in fields outside the town, and the grain was brought in after it had been threshed. Nuts, fruits and berries

▷ This beautifully carved wooden cart belonged to a Viking queen. Simple wooden carts with wooden wheels were a common sight in the streets of a Viking town. They were used to take goods to and from ships at the quayside, and to bring in food and other items from the surrounding countryside.

were gathered from the countryside, to add variety to the Vikings' diet. Cattle and sheep were kept outside the town, too. They were brought in to the town to be slaughtered and butchered when necessary.

Many Viking towns were built beside lakes or rivers or on the coast, and so fish was important to the people who lived there. Some of the fish was caught locally, but some was also brought in by ship from other areas. For example, barrels of salted herring were brought from Iceland to the quayside at *Jorvik*. They were exchanged for the grain which Iceland needed. The Vikings in Iceland could not grow enough crops, because the growing season there was shorter.

Cooking in towns

Most houses in Viking towns were smaller than those in the countryside. Often they had only one room, in which the entire family ate, slept and kept all their belongings. This room was usually dark, even in the middle of the day, as the Vikings did not know how to make glass for windows. Some houses had holes cut into the walls to let in the light. These

▽ These portable scales were used by Viking traders. They weighed the pieces of silver, which were often used instead of coins to pay for goods.

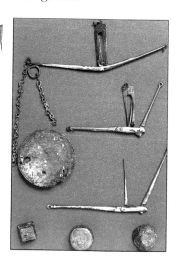

▽ One of the luxuries which Vikings in towns could enjoy was good quality wine. It was imported from the Rhineland, Germany, in pottery jugs like this one.

Index